THE AREA OF SOUND
CALLED THE SUBTONE

NOAH ELI GORDON

ahsahta press

Boise State University • Boise • Idaho • 2004

Ahsahta Press, Boise State University
Boise, Idaho 83725
http://ahsahtapress.boisestate.edu

Cover art: "Granulated Dreams" by Michael Labenz
Author photograph by Marcus DeMaio
Book and cover design by Janet Holmes
First printing December 2004
ISBN 0-916272-81-8

Library of Congress Cataloging-in-Publication Data

Gordon, Noah Eli, 1975-
The area of sound called the subtone / Noah Eli Gordon.
    p. cm.
"Winner of the Sawtooth Poetry Prize, 2004."
ISBN 0-916272-81-8 (pbk. : alk. paper)
I. Title.

PS3607.O5943A98 2004
811'.6--dc22

                    2004014345

Grateful acknowledgment is made to the editors and publishers of the following journals in which some of
these poems first appeared: Tom Orange at *2004 DC Poetry Anthology*; Vincent Standley, Hermine Meinhard,
and Andrea Baker at *3rd bed*; Jesse Seldess at *Antennae*; Ron Henry at *Aught*; Jim Behrle at *Can We Have Our
Ball Back?*; Sarah Campbell at *P-Queue*; Trevor Calvert and Michael Cross at *Syllogism*.

Thanks are also due to Michael Cross for challenging me to bring the dream sequence from "Jaywalking the
Is" into the world, and for the subsequent use of the first one in his "Secret Swan" public art project.

Thanks to Nick Moudry for a collaboration project which prompted the title poem.

Thanks to Christopher Reiner for publishing "Jaywalking the Is" as a chapbook in his Margin to Margin
series, and to Christopher Rizzo for publishing "What Ever Belongs in the Circle" as a chapbook on his
Anchorite Press.

FOR ERIC BAUS

CONTENTS

WHAT EVER BELONGS IN THE CIRCLE

hello the poem says make me a motor

no matter & I'll go all summer

humid just like the movies & you could do

for laundry walks other ways to kill

afternoon shapes like evening shapes

so marsupial or ginger in the fridge artificial

king of the middle rung getting stepped on

& steaming kale isn't such a breakthrough

but consider the supermarket book

gets you out of the house & into an intermittent sense

of what it means if free time dreams

a larger redemptive arena & dancing is just that

though you might break the continuity

just clause clause behind the space

keeps turning & out comes enough

moon flag eastern forest field guide sensibility

to spring up & catch one redundancy

you hold dearest as the phone pulls away

the ladder's pulled away & it's not so high

to climb past the principles a code of conduct

opaque as linen chores aren't their namesake

but to return money turning back

to procedural talk if the poem says

list your goals like goals are tangible & you could

have an emotional reaction as opposed to

one thinking through the writing or writing

through the thinking to call it a motor

running bareback without a horse

& chalking up inevitability obvious

or oblivious an avalanche

then recount the lives of your siblings

say my sister for whom a house is stability

& layering on poker face sole soliloquy

buried how long the carpet'll stay clean

when it's click click there's a ghost in the dust

overly self-aware of collecting from each

sliver a thing to call its own owning a future or not

some shadows look like spiders & there's a face

in the door & a face in the wall & hailing

nonchalance in a rush hour runway taxi time

next to the window ethically it's power

to pull the shade though shallow to narrate panaceas

honing in on the nest of hair in this comb

incubation outhouse near the little airport

next to the cornfields O it's another landing

how does that ghost know it's a ghost

& was the face a memory or did he really say

please open the shade if he's a fiction

& the shade's a stand-in for human innovation

who pulls the mimetic strings says hail to the grammarian

all I wanted was a syllable ghost window ghost walker

I'd rather write through the year of our bedsprings

a dual-consciousness plowing past the intellectual reaction

to a moving arm says can you type out the hum

rev up operative synaesthesia table what's on top is real

ivy in a real clay pot or a scant fiction figuring the distance

between a blurred mind & caustic reconfiguration

says better to water the plant than walk away

a stick stuck on telephone wires & a squirrel

point & say foreigner then harbor some hidden

myopic nerve-short & in a nanosecond

the squirrel knocks down the stick

knocking over the clay pot anticlimactic

airport dumb show pantomiming

the silence of a jet stream then parting the sky

with more runway runoff to an alchemical solution

diluted moon planetarium pulling the apogee

of orbiting insects like a bee ratchets by

& I'm all look out dangerous neon warning sign

the neighbors on the back porch

expect the walls to make a great & noble eater

of he who wants naked death pictorial

when an armored car rolls in & "the people"

wants its plug-me-in poem in the green room

with the tin ceiling the clock reads

geese overhead forging ambition

to be a lazy poster boy for deprogramming

80's sitcom & culturally isolate responders

to group think I thought we'd have more

in common than communal reading

instant message me to a real forest lifejacket ode

made a fine oar then water came up to our waists

triggering some lesser iconography Mike thought

making up your own saints but I could

just mention the actual days & you'd get

the blades of a box fan in the window

Masonic St. brick façade manifesto

O crosswalk high-beam us to the highway

pumped with sufficient song lyrics

to pad an ambulance heart whose landing pad

is a lighthouse am I self-conscious

to think my pockets are bulging

hand slapped for leaving the chopsticks upright

in lowbrow calligraphy lacquer a cardboard box

then punch me in the face the ugliest

in Gainesville proto-autobiographic zero hour

says trust the song not arbitrary ethnographic elevation

& the view from this cliff in the dark

like the dullest light ever to grace a candelabra

rent-by-the-hour motel Manhattan & Staten Island ferry

makes a mind pop twenty minutes afterward

the imp of tenacity puts a candle on his forehead

says the motor sounds off nervous system dispersal

she pats the heart pulse retro-day glow handprint

on an old t-shirt the worst way

to ask ex-stunt double for the afterlife

some aggressive blue jay wants to truth or dare us

to the white plains in a plain white shirt

butchering rhododendrons & I couldn't tell

an insect the size of a human

laying down vanity ascending birth canal

says everything on this mantle piece is a piece

of everything meaningfully ascribed

or momentarily stalled if I'd rather listen to Dead Prez

than get your hair did & alienate me alienate me

it's too comfortable in the country

to traffic in idyllic understatement dread costume

I won't comply with the blank wall admit the dream

where Peter brought the painting over in pieces

so soak me in some other solution

the camera eye wants a complementary mint

leaves the restaurant before crumbling

into inhospitable vacuum & he wants

all the shells I've collected & a sparrow

terrified by the tragedy of pita bread

call it duty so I can call in sick

return the questions asked

of a great tragedy upon Latin trees

moving bodies a vindicated radio

outside the garden turbulent phenomena

the sky terrible in wingspan arching over

an ideal ocean idiotically dented all night the waves

say marry me to a muscle make of me a prime mover

I'm proud of the lobsters

have seen Puerto Rico through the reeds

dressed in rust brick armor amassed

on the rooftops redolent firing squad mystique

slave to a copy machine syndrome

I'll succumb to the broken glass behind the hospital

an afternoon gloriously lost in new street-crossing signals

mesh with the hydrogenated mind

high fructose corn syrup catalyst

for the perfect human being wastes the most money

I make a pretty mime sound O free ticket

to a tour of this town's best alleyways

ollie to an upper atmosphere breastfed dystopia

or a simple line of ants in their wind-up orders

he wanted me to come over & unlock something

without basic principles in check

tracing the shape of the sand in the sand

& reading by clock radio light

makes impossible beauty I'll build her a new head

to hang all the extra necklaces on

next sharpshooter condemnation

next paint by numbers a lemon poem

if the outside world's a distraction

why not invent a new alphabet

animals do animal things in the dark

misanthropic tell-all tiny treasure inside a summer horse

the bells ring for no reason & we too

find an exercise in airing nothing of importance

impatiently tuning the alternate current

& we too advocate for bird things & rock things

tree things & things which are shallow clear

insatiable turbine vibration no root things

no masked things only things that rev vowels

no boards wedges levers picks

nothing in a nail nor that which floats

a stalemate landing pad insect fatigue

nothing edged or ambiguous

the bells ring for no reason & we too

refuse the sound of the slamming door

threshold things or trembling

already ruined crushed radioactive hotel

sonnet adjective more oil more road

the age of the undiminished human

either drone patio toothbrush buzz

barbed sound in bastard noise

& we too worship the choking air

around the circle the rectangle mounds of squares

& the mounting sense of geometric erosion

of global incongruity of monied things

the little frog stares an ignoble tacit entity

acrid absence of conceptual significance

the bells the bells bird things & rock things

O harpsichord upon the playground

things fit in my mouth pretty-like

kerosene musician infinitely doubled

I've picked the two of hearts & the ten of hearts

wheeling invisibility bees bees & teeth

I've picked an orange amplifier

the mosquitoes the horizon the casket

the harmonious skins blue hope blue valley

peck peck of tranquilized submission

so the octopus continues in its mystery

& the seasons half-heartedly continue

& the red motorcycles make us taller

& they want to take something else off

so we let them take something else off

& they want to tell us how they've taken it off

& we let them tell us how they've taken it off

& we call it structured

like your face is a shape I thought of

then couldn't stop the thought

but I want to show you how they danced

in the neighborhoods made birds a shrine

they have bells on their feet & mongoose gardens

pulled me out with forceps ask & I'll show the scar

a bleached thing is a dimmer light

O small o of disorder

move me along like we graze here

7/03

Sentences are not emotional but paragraphs are. I can say that as often as I like and it always remains as it is, something that is.

—Gertrude Stein, "Poetry and Grammar"

Chamber of Commerce or commencement speech lounging on the wrong subway line? Rather than a stranglehold to transcend the phone wares I'm sinking under, someone in an expensive hat calls his implicit contract the be-all-end-all motivational sublime, an ideal peach rotting in the over-saturated slide. If you promise to listen, I promise to undo the leash, de-lead the drywall. I'd say it's stylized dialogue but that'd be acting on bad faith.

I go on sensory overload outside, safer with the same room, same chair, star charts as nicks in the wall. The immobile scenery of what I'm missing out there fills me like a crow's nest, might as well carry a sign, grounding the play-by-play of someone passing on a cell phone or trying to embrace the pond by falling in. It's a construct as bad as plywood scaffolding, how the coins in my hand could muck it up halfway across the globe or keep me insular, forgetting what I said to whom, eyes plastered to the concrete as an excuse. Clouds overhead won't expand where the mind goes when I'm stuck striking the surface of a few puddles as obliquely as I do the shop windows. Rain on the sidewalk is rain on the ceiling & my suit is just right for the job.

I sloped into the American gold standard. Got all harlequin, shaved head, masked face, variegated tights, wooden sword. I was in a movie about movies, working the laugh track backwards, warming my hands by cupping the few ounces of ash left from the workhouse skirmishes, some paregoric to down the playpen syndrome. I'd rather be anesthetized than another Peter Pan statistic. Dukes up. Dogs out. Call it a clinical cynicism, the fear of white suits in a well-lit room, the fold between waking up without enough air to ease the straps off & ODing without ever leaving the left-brain, right-brain paradigm, apart from a stroll to the pawnshop, & of course, it's closed. Admittedly, I need the night to make my mask worth its weight.

Habitation tempers the dial tone I inhabit, hoarding the earpiece & priceless circuitry when you walk into yourself. The route is a fig & the archer's fingers make two good body parts for every trained hero hoping to salvage a little personal space. They want their own ink to overdo it, their own half-submerged retro-stylings. Every shirt in the shop is for sale, even the one the owner's got on. Starboard, a little sparrow choking on its diminutive song. Aft, the laughing hyenas in their best rope-trick come-on lines. I'd mention the open carcass if the smell hadn't handled that one already, if I hadn't been hanging up for at least half an hour.

Gunship grunts. Splendid assemblage & cinnamon acetaminophen. The glue holds the gutters in. The rhetoric's a loose-leaf apprentice. Cracks in the oracular self I'm splitting open, splicing states of consciousness onto what? Locomotive sound wings? A burnt rabbit in the trap & a rabid set of number laws the numb part of me knuckles up to. Tell it to the sludge, the oil slick, the slippage ousting us from Ollie-Ollie-oxen-free central. I've got a drawer full of keys that bend by themselves. Magic Realism, mute narration or just plain jack-in-the-box psychosis?

Gut rot in the gulfs, a way to ride the terror talk, risk the trenches. I'm in robes, ribbed. The last Saxon in starlight starting up a fresco for the toothcomb squad. & it's not the brandy I'm after, not the bolted door left open, a paradox under the urge to kick 'em down when every car sprays the street in your face. A bit to the back, head drooped, heart saying: that song comes every hour; those shoes match the treads I meant to follow. The tracks lead straight out of town & the bus brings it all barreling back, receipts, recipes, other groundhog days when the ground's so frozen nothing save contempt would risk a soliloquy to the few stems still leaning toward the fading light. It's cold enough in valediction alley to see your own breath shadowed along the pavement. Pulling teeth or retching from the plaster cast. There's a perfect mark under me & I'm pure bull's-eye for putting it there.

Photo of sand & standard philosophy, two threads to follow the room's line of reasoning. Along one we carried buckets, collected water, called the bridge an inevitability of architecture, figured a flame begins by repeating its name: catalyst, coffer, coffin. With the other we watched the dancer give in to gravity, a slow descent to the lowest point possible on the floor. To collapse or calculate what came out as a tickertape message through the outdated technology of an offhand allusion, she moved upstage, said, "Spiders make web light less comfortable, but limelight?" The weave of the dance was all the more remote since its curved pathways caused a weakened movement to accentuate the lack of space. Winter ends. Laughter happens downstage; it's the most visible form of motion.

Is there a border along the blatant moves? A way to approach the solitude protecting a personal dictum? "No TV when the sun is out," says Chatty Kathy playing computer chess. A dark & unflinching cultural collision would spread code pink in such abortive silence. Popular discontent or profound weariness? The pipeline disappears. The appearance differs, depending on a vantage point. Every fiction carries its own laws, crawls along the tall grasses, careful not to move against the wind. A broken pattern or a beacon to those who are watching? If you break a glass you've got more than when you started. If you pull the cord, the bus might stop the talking doll.

To say sleep works by accumulation is to disregard the weather in my head.

It makes a genius of the pillow, an apt anthropomorphic redundancy.

When the story stumbles into its fearless costume & everyone at the edge of the woods is worried their waiting-room bravado won't open to anything but the same door on the same house that seemed a little off in the morning, every anecdote has an empty object.

When your own name's written on the gate, negation is just something we do.

What's redundant about the human personal? The urge to cull an animal pronoun from a procession of wedding guests?

At least reductive absolutes rivet you somewhere closer to the actual rainfall, adjudicating ultimatums or handling the ounce of mulch it takes to cover any experience worth calling tactile.

There's nothing sharp about a knife in a movie.

& doesn't it make you fearless & brave to say so.

Think-tank spillage alters the facts I'm after & I'd rather the library weren't so loaded as the shame in all those fuses you couldn't connect to anything worth calling apocalyptic. Let's discount the landscape before trying to recreate it, since it's a lie to say knotted trees in the park lend a soapbox hair-trigger to the lamplight back here. It's bad enough they call you a seer when nomenclature is about the last thing you're bound to bridle. The mistakes move me in classic grace, hammering into Russia without keeping the rearview in check or hoarding unsent letters in hopes of gilding the filing cabinet into a predawn standoff. One side has me up in arms, the other about as empty as seats rising in tiers around the arena this afternoon couldn't help but construct. Who wants to be a contender if it's heartstrings they're vying for? I've got my private instruments & I'll keep them that way.

Someone's always upping the ante, a veritable snowfall on every horizon, an alternatively bound & unbound book I left on whose bus? Riding around what city? Seems I'm coming to terms with the upstairs neighbors, a musical variant for the not-so-perfect-pitch vocal runs I'm out of breath after. The afternoon dents itself into evening, although there's not much difference there. Maybe you make a salad, think about sliding into the next big motif. Later, there's dust in the water, holes I hadn't remembered digging, hands I thought I left alone. Sure, the police mean something, but five-card stud isn't any better than a solitary wiretap when the panhandlers pick you out of the crowd. I left the belt & I'm living the buckle.

Scraps of where the ladder scraped. A shard on a yellow sheet. Asking what airship parts a wing point's lingering fear of flight or asking if the channel switch people still switch channels. I'd considered moves, differing modalities, considered disassembling the battleship followed by a visit to the bait shop. If there were an object to stare into, something to refract the fixation of these dubious pluralities, well, the hounds would find home that much more fitting, curled at the edge of the bed. Bone-worn indignation? Another stick tossed into the hedge maze? I walked a mile trying to count as high as I could, but got lost on both accounts. Things freeze, I've said that before. The laundry is one constant you can count on. Turtle dove, where's my extra queen? I've got a 1,000 piece puzzle in mind & a few hours to grind.

Because we've internalized the king's horsemen, set the blade beside a tuft of grass, soaked a sprig of lavender in almond oil, seen paint congeal, bubble & flake, perfect chairs in perfect rows empty of perfection & the form a body takes when a folded curtain in a dresser drawer is shaken out & draped over an open door, like a single thought held as a hammer posed over the nail too bent to fasten anything but the sketched outline of a wooden horse hung above the fireplace, I can always say I'm full of saddles, that they'd stretch to fit any formal occasion, sway back & forth, & if I'm lucky, lull me to sleep.

To hinder potential or hold a bit of the broken-off houseplant, the bureaucracy involved in recounting an anecdote becomes clear. One needn't pass an outside character into an otherwise mimetic account. The mice were real mice, although the room was fictional, complete with one piece of furniture & the scent of rosemary. Working on the senses compounds the ease with which I'm able to repel an inadvertent impression of longing. It's not until you leave that the walls become a tangible barrier. Although every bank teller has a face, some hide their hands more easily. When there are other ways to call oneself an animal, I often wonder what the value of absolutes brings to any exchange, what the burden of hooves over paved avenues balances.

4:24 pm & I'm coming apart gracefully. One hand half-resembling the cookbook, the other held in a half-completed mock salute to the disposable camera left in the backseat of a stranger's car. The best thing about living with someone is the best thing about wheels—they spin. It's algebra we're getting at. Me, writing it down, you working equations into the economy revolving around every photograph I've ever taken. So the Renaissance seems overused & calling it a historical fiction won't add any flange to your effects pedal. The forest is there. Let's keep it that way.

Does mythic entitlement wash out our diseased vectors? It's like reading a book of reason to splice what was missing from my daily routine back onto its alphabetic appendage, the arm I couldn't help but slide under the pillow, there being no other way to straddle the line between a comfortable sleep & waking with one eye crusted over, regardless of where I meant to see myself in the future tense, turning a log to watch insects scamper or nostalgic for the fireplace shown in an automobile advertisement. Eldridge Cleaver at large, setting a price when you can't make out the fine print, then finding proof in diligent fear making a joke of the fact handlers. Did the snow-covered bird's nest outside the bay window lead to another telephone solicitation list? A correlative for English teatime? I suppose I could ask questions all afternoon, but who among the is would hear? After all, angel is a dangerous verb & there's a dust storm inside the little spider I just saw. It's the same brand I killed yesterday, part noise cloud, half raw denunciation.

That's one way to subjugate what you can't saddle, seed the Cloud of Unknowing to speed-read yourself through another fuzzy-diced measure of divinity. Immediately preceding the subjective, the jar of mixed nuts, the jackhammer trance & miniature peach blossoms, tethered to unwanting a place to work on the recurring sound of crushed glass & the liquid taking its shape for granted. I'd say it's analogous to this growing collection of plush animals, which don't correspond to anything in the actual world—stuffing is stuffing. Care to call the tautology squad? I think the birds woke me up before, but I'm willing to risk an alternative beginning. Today I'm wearing a red sweatshirt. Tomorrow I think I'll wear it too.

SECOND DREAM

To say what gives a landscape orchestration is a sure way to flower too soon.

Can you sister a house without seasons? Wait on the anonymity of a single tree in bloom?

If it's grace you're after here's the first of my faults:

I still believe it takes something sharp to cut one down.

There are tiers to every state of presence & we blossom in real time, along with the outfits that outlast us.

So the dancers are dressed appropriately, does that make motion any more meaningful?

I'd take back the music's forked-tongue if gifting were a silent art.

Besides, there's no such thing as a symbol, right?

I hung a picture over the counter, held numbers in my head. I was calculating, nearly contorted into a space large enough for slips & shifts, the slight nuances of refraction, gold-glints & garlands, Town Square's ineffectual geometry, crossed streets & the crossing of streets, where one defends a sense of direction as insatiable though unsettled, while the numbers won't line up in their proper order, the perspective I had in mind when setting off, or the mud still clinging to the shape my shoes made. How far is it from the footprints to the heart pulse? We agree on sentiment, no? Well, then why all the gloss, all the gross overstatements when a simple chair could offer one a place to sit?

The reluctance of continual backtracking & the angle of light along the floorboards & an insistent calling or something appropriately labeled "luxury" to brood over the plastic trees we'd feel slightly more comfortable around. The teller at the bank is one way to say line up your amenities before the bullet-spark finds my favorite coat draped over my favorite chair in the worst place one would want to live. A list of mistrusts or a lisp misting luck? It's only one's self-aggrandizement anyhow. The butcher, the baker, the automated factory three blocks from here. If something breaks, call it broken. There's a math to every trust factor, a vertex to each angled list. She winks & I think she means it. Interpretation? Astral Blaster? Everything sounds like a band name when you rummage through a dictionary of architectural terms.

Being afraid to articulate a position is one way to put up your dukes in a knock-'em-down template. The framework of conversational inaccuracies accumulates wealth to leash a list of my favorite quotes by the not-quite-famous. I'm never as aphoristic as I seem & all the shiny magazines make it all the more unmanageable. By now trumpets are playing taps without us, & since I tossed my one-night-stand paperback of aberration in the back alley, someone else'll have to dog-ear the exact spot where Lear's gone cliffside.

Grime in the book begets grime in the book when language is the worst kind of equal sign to set sail under. To suffer in the pastoral sense isn't half as enlightening as having your hands tied behind your back when you didn't even ask for a massage, just a message to bow-up the gift-box deliverance another free object brings to an unseen expense. Adjective traffic backs us all up, but what did you expect? A litmus test in the Laundromat? Chinese food with a European flare & an American eye toward innovation? Everyone has a haircut, some just hope you can tell.

Under what engine rides an earth or a gear of it? Plastic in the heart is plastic in the heart & remaining helpless isn't an option for the valuating marionette or the weight of possibilities under the pressure of manipulative dogma. It's taken its place beside the massive guiding hand above the turnstile. Just out of earshot, under what engine rides an officious fake or a taxi back to it? To utilize the material in such a way that's instructive to one's own work, or to own an airplane without so much as an inch of runway, an ounce of fuel or a fragment of flight experience, could kill the heroic simile inside perfectly balanced plain hills the painting displayed in the foreground.

Plot an escape route for the fallacies of such a quiet century & mud clings to the edge of the day. Homecoming is reserved for those having somewhere else to get to. Joy & arrival not as sequential as their buoyant similarities, stuck in traffic as an overdose, an anodyne also. So we poison one another & call the flag the feel of daily tasks in diluted certainty— the morning so muscular it skips past itself, never quite as adjustable as it seems. West of here, nothing happens & we love each other for it, for our forest sentimentality & enough fresh water fish to stock an infinite number of painted lakes. My house holds hundreds of me. Give each a quiver & the hunter's half-way to the amphitheater. Emptying the locks. Opening the rocks.

There are victims there & their victims are there, undressing ceaselessly. What comes in droves often doesn't. The pinewood. The scattering mice. The tiny noose in my shirtsleeve. The thin water. The light in the field. The scattering mice. The tiny noose they share. My shirtsleeves rolled to the elbows. The desk. My hands on it. The mice underneath. The light through the field. The thinly lit room. My hands on the desk. The overwhelming sound of someone breathing. The window. The pines outside. The field. The dented bucket. Someone breathing. The miniature rope. The knots in it. The fibers. The flaws.

Seductive obscurity chains one to the marrying bell without turning an abstraction into any more of an entity than if one were to find me in a mauve beret leaning a little too close to the counter story lurking just beyond the now fading edge of what could have been an entry point for some minor character to climb out from the wreckage left after the dogs had arrived to the hurried shouts of still other would-be scavengers salvaging what they felt I had ignored upon entering into such a state-sponsored union where the sound of the links being pulled taut didn't tame anything save the desire to continue down the same cobbled street next to the remains of what had previously been perfectly reflective glass.

To say the body makes its own background music would be rambling.

It hooks you in a gentle way, this I-think-I-can engine from the book I'd hand you if I had a book out here.

Think, vistas of despair for any Johnny-on-the-spot snow machine.

Think, lungs work even while you're in bed.

Is a boom mic a symbol?

Maybe I'm being romantic, but if someone's wearing diaphanous robes I'd hope for a hide-behind-the-curtain bureaucrat to bail me out of the five-minute break inside such boring weather.

Think, forest for the trees or how far out your own hand seems when it's the furthest point between two lines.

So the geometry hyenas gear up, circle a few times before settling down, before swallowing the requisite crumbs in such a quiet homecoming.

A locket's job is to quell motion. Simple enough that I crush the spider in the book I'm reading before it gets halfway to the floor. Shuffled pages, dead bolts, dormitories. Even the museum's got a final solution a few vertebrae shy of the full skeleton, a redundant mask for the amateur masquerading mosaic-choppers. I should've argued for a simplicity that, while appearing to be loosely based on sincerity, is largely the work of crisscrossing, still visible tracks of birds above the dissipating snow banks. It melts because you let it. Every note, wanting an engine, an organ to cauterize the chord. You walk into a force field but it's not special—it's huge. You draw an S, then a more different S, unable to own syntax. Things are things & one hopes they're happy.

Someone's fascinated by the context her paintings take on the first time they're hung together. Someone can't afford to leave a tip, just walks out. Someone's far from finished with the paper, legislating geography then lapsing into dull twilight. It's arrogantly idyllic, the method acting that makes more of the stage than who's on it, the moment when asking the music box if it dies like this every day moves one's affinities closer to the waiter than the museum worker. There's a metaphor about nature, art & menus I meant to plug in here, but I'd rather leave the carnival of stargazer lilies with its own distinct smell.

Every disaster has an endgame, the broom against the slats spreading wider as domesticity ages the barn's red paint. The sky, not so dominant as we'd have liked when the only time without shoes is spent in bed & the nightstand is a nightstand. You practice a little, blow through the spit valve, remember how easily hematite breaks. If there's a heart to every mammal, something about gestation inside, a lineage that's intrinsically wired, un-worked at, more rhythmic, ambulatory, an exposed metronome, the minutiae of time it takes for the mallet, having landed on the string, to register a sound, not a sound but the expectation of it, how it lingers, how we brace for the terrific accidents, the beautifully undone anatomy book, its cover worn through in spots, slight lines of white, subtle abrasions, the weight of a lock of hair & the weight of its intention, a question slowing the essence of movement, turning the wheel to the right, bringing the blood back to its roadhouse, a decoy mediation beyond ulterior motives, a dead civilian in the dirt, a photograph of his shirt.

Was it wondering on faith, or with faith, that a slight change in the record of my doubt could crush the staircase through an idle landscape? Weather, almost as boring as architecture & the persistent drumming in my kidneys while the screen slows, dialogue taking a backseat, a common focus for these overindulgent pleasantries. One side of going out makes us witness the other, loosening a shoelace to avoid the suitable dinner plate. In watercolor, the problem is clarity. Calling it pop-art isn't good enough. There were times when waiting for the film to end was more appealing. I've got to believe in something other than absolutes or intellectual abstractions. It hurts how insular everything feels in a rainstorm, how the wobble of wolfsong was the only thing they addressed the union with.

How do you carry the dailyness of it & still render a dust storm. There was chatter from the bellows. We passed a dairy farm, an outdoor well, things that exist for us as tactile perception—things piled under their expectations. I feel awful about my new shoes & the love I harbor for them. We make different excuses, carving the authentic present into the bark of a sagging birch. I'll attest to being outmoded, to the bruises that chastity belt brought on. A justifiably pure phenomenon is just out of touch.

If the expressivities of the human face are mirrored in the eyebrows of dogs, if they learn because we tell them to, if someone fills out an application in a few minutes, lands a job, makes dinner, dreams herself an ownership, then are we stealing from or assembling one another? Used-up nation, here's my new riding saddle. It was too late to answer the phone. Often, I'd rather say it differently, turn it on the exchange, the progress of another week's clemency. Feathers in the flowerbeds? I'm not exaggerating, look at how high the house is.

Mathematically speaking, floodgates braced, facial rudiments in full view, I'm more than a door between the Arabic number for last in line and the length a kite will go before the string is completely taut. Wind was a factor, swept water another. And what are the koan slingers doing now, field wiring? Once the train arrived, no one dared to stand. We didn't want to appear overly eager, unjustly relieved. I was fingering the novel in my coat sleeve, worried it would slip out, wondering if the others were as tense as how I'm sure I must have seemed. Dotted line. Pencil lore. Is it wrong to ask for a difference between done & finished, an already is?

You can cinderblock the dead city, dilute it with ink, with a fine-toothed comb, some character dust in the day play. It's hard being a drama hound, cradling luck, shelving the days into a warehouse—a holding dock without a working lock. Time passes or thickens or falls from a jar. Never anything as exciting as someone on a window ledge, but maybe it's a good sign. Maybe cartography's the way to go. When were maps more useful, after you learned to dance or before your first loss lesson? & when would that cocktail alter the works? The band takes requests from the bandstand. What figures, from anybody's guess.

To say thunder only happens because we believe we hear it is one chord I'd strike if I weren't holding such a broken instrument.

So there's a light in the distance—why bother pointing it out?

Indirection is its own worst enemy.

& speaking of echoes, I'd place those footfalls far enough behind me that being followed means a circle is one way to walk out of the story.

If every dog has his day, does repeating something make it seem more appropriate?

Death head, death hand, death heart, now the myth's getting a little octane, an apologia outside the outline traced by a worn down crayon.

Do we still leave the light on when we're not home?

Do movies stop time or did I just read that somewhere?

I've got eight minutes in the dunk tank, a fundamental being-in-the-world, everydayness covering the uncanny like clouds above the asphalt, the shadow a bouncing ball makes. Follow? A coat caught on a nail comes off, constitutes an oblivious sort of order. Could the clients be any less electrifying? The lighthouse out of range? Phone dash. Felt lace. American memory wears a lawsuit. Tailor me an hour without something to fill, white sheets or red curtains. What else is useless as an elephant gun? A century of green leaves or some leftovers? A general ontological characterization of conscience? Gesundheit! How can you be humble, living all your wilderness with the backdoor left open.

Articulating despair or articulation of despair in the dishes needing to be done. I rubbed the image from so much excess. The screen porch where love is childlike & receding. Thursday followed by another Thursday & they arm themselves like that. A slender arm in the foreground. Who doesn't have a body to harness willful redemption, a handmade atlas of the world? These illustrated pictures have taken their gloves off & wait in the living room for the artist to arrive. Sketch me in here. I've been hiding all morning.

The graphite flakes off, leaves marks where I hadn't intended. Fingerprints on a phone book or a catalog of the afternoon's complication. Is there a partner to self-deification, a pattern in how we navigate each other's resistance? Suddenly could be the sorriest adverb to wrench the assembly line to a halt. I'd considered calling it a day, but there were still echoes to unchime. Bees encoded in bushes encoded in bronze work ending in the probability that an event will occur, given that another has or will do so.

If terror cake seems too cute, why not try extending the idea; everything orbits its own frequency, turns back at some point. If you're lucky, it'll burn with the woodpile. If you're waiting, try to relax. A firm persuasion can remove mountains & redundancy makes for efficient advertising. Here money fish, how 'bout a harness? I hadn't given much thought to the framework of morpheme thinking. Tick, tick, goes the mouse. Tick tick, goes the house. Although it's enough to crack manifest destiny's guardrail, the coastline couldn't stop us from swerving into such an untranslatable world. & we're under water anyway.

I'm taking my pirate ship apart. An overdose on the letter arrival circuit? An accidental gift? I tried to drop & roll, putting out what I though was a flame in the fridge. January day. January dance. January doldrums. Let's talk about baseball on the TV. January sprint. January seal. January seventh. Let's talk about baseball on the TV. January error. January elevator. January exam. Let's talk about baseball on the TV.

You pick it up, play it & put it back. Is that funny? My person has a theme. Thermodynamics & sediment rotation. I unrolled the dream of a city without its back draft, then tore the sheets in two, hoping for some fresh air to lift off the lingering smell of old books. My person also has a green library, a gutting knife & some tinsel. We go out, all of us, carrying a picture in the wallet for precisely such an occasion. If the floorboards creak, someone's walking. This is how we do it. Like this & like that & like this & a.

Waiting for the fossils to thaw was one thing. Maybe I shouldn't have torn the wooden horse from your library, ridden it bareback into New England's need for another castle. Regardless, the splinters made an appropriate mantelpiece to mark the Dionysian affirmation of all these empty bottles; besides, the lessons said to pull from the root before puncturing the lids. Let's hope there's enough breathing room in those ballet slippers to start the wind chimes signifying. You can play the clown in your best halo, but don't take my word for it—there's an expert to unwind all the false-prophet-in-a-tinder-box posturing that passes through the noun machine.

Someone buys cigarettes & someone is me. Don't you love the clarity vectors over the flow chart, the union suit I was lost in? The strings matched the sea gown, scrapped, scuttled, tore a wing from our tonnage vessel, our towering blue vicissitudes. Changing my clothes everyday is one answer, static drips another. I could proceed in the normal fashion, go with the go-getter label. Lettuce soup. Long dot. Dints. Smile when you enter a room, someone might listen to the largess.

To say the locomotive moves from effect to outcome historicizes the distance between a pile of coal & the vegetable dye drying into an animal shape on some porous stone.

There's nothing philosophical about a flat surface & suffocation is the art of listening to flowers age.

If the century of synaesthesia died inside the combustion engine, does labeling oneself a social realist make sleep any more palpable?

Does thinking about a piano have a sound?

Does a museum organize anything besides our own death?

Does it change the way the real world looks?

A poem about a movie about a dream about a painting is about all I can project.

It takes something sharp to cut off an appendage.

Expectation week wounds the suggestion box, makes the indefinite duration the Great Knowers of Suchness play in seem less a continual present than a constant clock sparring. It's the unconceptualized event I'm after; it's pens, springs, transistors; it's rallies, dirt oxen, noise doves; it's lemon grass, wires, physical proximity; it's culling the lap sack, rain, carbohydrate formulation; it's exposure to sun light, decking the always, lifts, bottles & the blinding ray of light in the casket. If you have a headache, drink water. If you remember nightclubs, shuffle your hatchet. It could hack through a phone book in half the time.

I'm all Camelot when the cognition folders do their thing. Rain in their outfits or reign in their outfits. It's a fitting underling I'm after as the day splays like a scalp-lock, a tuft of hair left to challenge the contrast of light & shade. Okay, the Dutch painter's a shoe-in, but how many bulbs charge in the winter, sprout in the weaves? Lecture me a terrible Asian stew, I'm ready to learn more than semantic drills, looking for some bells in my realism gear. A destitute plagiarizer along the spelling breakout? An occasional fine cook? Enough about me, when are the red hotels coming home?

I don't think in shredder games or sound jumps, putting a plow out front to give a little clearance to the tango plantation. How do you prove you're a hired hand when they've mangled your in, synthesized your as? It's a mother-dear dilemma for a fifteen-minute browser to palm the commonwealth in such a chilling tea set. Behind the facts, a faceless whistle. My apologizes, as I once cut the tendon in my pinky & now harbor an actual fear of knives. It's not surprising. Everyone reads on the subway. Take my briefcase, I'm done evicting the border patrol. Dynamite, dynamism, or dinosaur? Don't get me wrong; I'm talking about ownership. It's an objective world.

All this surface play attests to the attraction of the character-sketch crowd, the game-face vendors. Danger marionette, where's your smile now? There's that bus terminal a block from my apartment & there's bound to be a better way to arrive at some depth, to clear the frequencies, defuse the knowledge that follows a range finder. Dressed in yellow to mark the New Year, it's a quake I'm after. Tugging on the ropes one writes in won't materialize anything attached to the end. The ant continues in its idiocy. I'll leave it there.

The way things worked was by harvesting potentiality. I could say I had a point, was made from a series of gradually smaller picture frames. I could say global hygiene turns the candle works loose. Rewired. Relayed. Relapsed. If there's a resin to varnish this synthetic echo, the lowest point on a calendar grid, will the day take itself for granted, wait in the wings for an operatic discharge from the x I forgot fill in. Dress me in a skirt if you like, I've been to Kentucky, been working things by turns. Perhaps it's the point that makes the picture.

Machine me animal. I have a shiny rock collection. It's all timbre, scrolling in the scarf wares to compose a factory from the theme's first note. If there's a sharp edge, I'd cancel those predictable replies they print on tracing paper, crumble the excess screws over someone else's bicycle ambience. Moving toward balance? The soul of money? An infinite circle's power of intension? I'm getting good at the new wage thing, call it love for the winner instead of the race. A jet takes off. Pointing out the obvious is a cruel sort of shakedown.

If everything tends to move toward its original desire, does ivy share the mushroom's night stalking? It's snowing inside the kill switch. Brushing a dry reed against the still wet oils of an unfinished painting, or brushing a dry reed against the still surface of the lake, or loving the way I knew you'd read the morning & its ubiquitous flares away. What's a practical dream anyway? The dust, settling gratuitously. Me, in my desert shirt.

Contingency is one way to measure where the fake opens, where the house then the horse takes up the entire frame. Famous people are falling in love everywhere & I'm admittedly under the weather inside both scripts, the fake copy & the faux original, the first sentence & its elusive tail between its legs. Later, two small, opaque spheres appear on the film, the light filtered through before registering it as a mistake. In cinema, it's called crying the bird shadow, an utterance understood as the urge to say what one's profession prevents. In Italy, it's called the bull casket. If you drink from it, it hums.

SIXTH DREAM

To say the instant has an aftermath overlooks the long-haul endgame of a minute's self-renewal.

Clocks are responsible for themselves.

Mirrors are responsible for themselves.

Tides are responsible for themselves.

There's no such thing as a chemical reaction.

The earth moves in reverse.

If there were a moral to replace each circuit, a recalcitrant thread dangling far enough from the original weave one could pull apart the argument & keep the net intact, the unpolished crown pushed under the bed, out of reach, so that only the mice could breed a kingdom worth naming, a few well-wishers for the nostalgic derision of a parking-lot hierarchy, where space is reduced to absurdity & even the color red seems washed of its connotations— a blank slate blocking out the market-driven economy implicit in such nomenclature fallout, then tell me something I don't already know.

A clock is an empty object, as is an ocean.

I took to the still breathing like translation shots. A beautiful vista, shimmering in the dark below the original. What's a name when you're dead in a fish barrel, when you're born in Tennessee. I could have added an adjacent line to the unfinished map, a prime adjective, something to envelope the progression. For every blueprint there's another possibility, an alternative text outside the color wheel. The temperament insects gain a hand, but the game flatlines before folding. Turning on the rain, the rust, the rosy hue of a particular sunset's inevitability, the analogy drains the copy. I'm stuck with a chain dragged along the pavement or a pack of what might be wolves, their silhouettes threading through the mountains in the left-hand corner of the screen.

I was waning in the owl light, half expectant, half excess. The door slammed. The diggers dug. I did the adverb thing. My sewing hand in the hots & hoping to out-freeze those debutante hysterics. If there's a red switch you should flick it. If there's a car outside, think payback buckles, bright coinage, flint ambivalence. It could crumble in the other tide, could tear the oldest fig from the trees. I found them in a dead book, in a daybook, in the Book of When. There's always a crayon to draw a straw house beside the ransacked village. If I'm a helper, well, take this stethoscope. It's too hot in the dregs anyhow.

You could say I'm trying to find another setting on the wherewithal dial. The diatribes meant well, but what's a polemic to a pacifist when the stakes are too worn to set these Dostoevskian dictations to an outdoor comeuppance. You describe a haircut by its shape, listen to the London horse if you must. The landing pads at least offer a reluctant end to this hemoglobin holding cell, to someone calling home from the hornet's nest. Why walk downtown when there are other cities burning?

So prone to violation, the telephone walls in another king-come-lately. The sound shuffles the walls inward. I considered moving to a different city, sold most of my clothes instead. Stockpiling the backwater brings out the mauve in my idea of a meaningful radius, the distance between my first film role & the last time I walked past a window without looking at my watch. There's a haze in the outhouse. I wonder if they could breed the recipe box with your lingering sense of a sentimental breakdown. If it's my serious face you want, just ask. When I said I could turn any mirror inward I think I was lying. When the gun went off in the first act I knew I'd gotten it backwards, blown the finale on a cutout-bin biography of some actor no one recognized anymore.

Above the groundswell, above the lamplight, above the brooding sense of an opposite direction I could have gone, above the wind, above the ocular presence of all the other audience members, above the hillside, above the lack of a landscape template, above the temperature it takes to melt the pages together without actually burning the book, above the sliver of tooth, above the clouds, above the already wavering alphabet, above the page, the book, the predetermined past tense, birds in awkward formation, a few still in the trees, a few stuck in the allegory.

Did I over-apply the stasis angle again, cancel the option to throw the soldiers an alternative ending? Sure, I got off the train no problem, but who knew the augurs would hold their own weather? If it's a windy day there's always another war on. The ropes wouldn't stop anyone from clocking in & my timecard dreams are about as catchy as a noose. I think I'll slide the blame down some other sideline, study the flight patterns of birds over the stadium. There's an awful omen in every animal's entrails, & to tell the truth I'd open myself expeditiously.

So a song turns the nearness sour & I'm either looking at that tree outside or staring at the wall. Neither helps me with the science in my colored fear, since trying to add another wing to a sailing vessel won't stop the water from leaking. What's a placid form of abstract eroticism anyway? I could look at pictures & wonder if the window's a savior inside a still conception, wonder if I was never good at painting because my hands were more cloyingly immobile than my heart. If you leave out the backdoor, make sure to run down the anvil. More specifics? How 'bout how heavy this hammer is.

I wouldn't call myself a conduit for that all-fours-as-a-way-to-show-one's-humility circuit. If you insist, the walnut opens. Someone brings in a plate of food & you're always hurtful, not that I meant to shove the needle into a blunt forbearance. What's in the basement is underneath & I think grand pronouncements are a little suspect. Who's in love with the dirt clown anyhow? I was clawing at it all afternoon, coming in without the cards, guilty of returning to the same theme, grass not being a yard until you project some order onto the individual stalks. Look at all those wires! I think my bookcase must be broken.

To say an image automatically strains for transcendence trumps the urge to inhabit the absence of meaning.

If you want to beat me over the head, wait till I'm dressed for it.

Horns are sharp objects.

Horns are also empty appendages.

If you're only didactic in the daylight, the confidently delusional telephone game, where someone tells you about it, because enacting is better left to the overstatement of dandelions bound to appear as the proverbial meat of the matter, then cannibalism could foreshadow the way we're always stealing from one another.

Fire bad, the obvious analogy.

Obviously, over saturation leaves us a little wet, leaves someone wearing a suit the clouds won't respond to accordingly, leaves a set of dictums you could ring out for the few drops of liquid it takes to call it a lake instead of a puddle when you're working on such a microscopic scale.

Should've had more torque in my love for the light switch.

The deer is slightly off balance. The moon is slightly embraced. The day is slightly abundant. The house is slightly tangible. The door is slightly aware. The field is slightly parallel. The noise is slightly present. The storm is slightly impending. The clock is slightly constricted. The fan is slightly immobile. The kitchen is slightly adjacent. The music is slightly fading. It's unlikely the classroom holds sway in a blank interval. It's unlikely the conscious dogs could help. The deer is slightly musical, but so is the sound of internal combustion.

Can the calendar make you slave to a glimmer of hair through the stained glass window? So, self-conscious simulacra, if you cross the street, cross the street. Simple dentistry when the heartquake's read in Braille, when the rhythm's heard clearly & each beat is wielded into the walking life we're after, into the riders I thought would add that adventurous touch. It's a beach day after all & I think I might hear the tides coming in. Losing the pulse? Well, counting backwards starts with collegial precision.

Splay the drainage angles. Call it a red tunnel toward grandiose nowheresville, a trace of the tusk storm, mystery in button-down fervor & cavalier shingles. I'm letting the first round end without a flicker of the already worn tasks, waiting to beat this dash into fine pumice—a firehouse discharge. Not to overestimate my pokerface, but I didn't listen when you said we're always grafting something, coasting a millennial disposition or talking with a full mouth to the false sun in a charcoal print covered with pinpricks. I could put objects anywhere, but it doesn't mean you should follow. The moon is an object & who wants a jarful of that ghost house? If there's no welcome mat, your guess is as good as mine.

Spider veins, beehive handles, what won't scare off an encroaching storm over the small lake in our anonymous painting? Imagine being obsessed with nuclear power when the candles singe a digger moth to bits. It's less than a willing host to the parasitic summary of the I you thought I'd let slip, unable to barnacle anyone, what with being prone to self-induced epileptic fits in your costume. Wind on. Wind off. The weather'll wear down the book faster than its freight circles. I'm consigned to a stitch of the story, pulled from the glossed finish radiating those wolf whispers. The master is always dying. Getting his shirt off is the hard part.

The disc shape in a dim sarcophagus midnights the song I walk into tuneless & an orange table covers the outline of evening tides. There's a chord to every backward motion, a lake house springing from the want for more vacation time. I've raised an animal fist, cracked the mast down the middle & left the flack battered in my darkroom gear. It's about gusting the intake, drawing the core rods from a brittle molten voice & congealing the choir's atmosphere. Some sounds break all boundaries, but what does bone music wear?

& I'm as sure of it as I am of the hour falling to pieces, little bits of brown string & a century of happenstance melodrama. What's precious in tundra circles won't keep the glove compartment closed, won't add an antique briefcase to another business clone. Everyone with something to sell, a board needing a straight face, an unbalanced hedgerow & paint pulled from the planks, a higher conditional in place, a visible river of dust, a passenger car, us relaxing into lunchtime. & with twigs still to collect! I could say it's a matter of replacing the hunter-gatherer mystique with a more tangible notion of how I should handle a mirror, but these are only my minor flaws. Please don't fail them.

If to feign a chance encounter is to fall out from an unbook, then is there allegiance without an actual subject, or, for that matter, anyone to remember when the clock became the centerpiece to an otherwise drab parlor-room distinction? It's not about entertaining, rather, a catalyst for how a few hours could waste into an evening of metallic clouds drifting over an irreconcilable museum-hall affair. An ode for passing cars, other landscapes I might have found myself in. So the dents show as easily as the stains & I'm hard pressed to do anything but continue in the alien corn.

Where are the platinum shimmers in such a catastrophe? The variegated notches in the corkboard I wrote in? It fell just the same, revealing the referents to keep from cashing out. Everyone more concerned with getting the day over, hoping it would loop back to a garlanded afternoon. There are table settings and the same few anecdotes around which I felt a sense of childlike wonder. Funny enough to realize what happened, what without anyone to phone during the rainstorm. The huddlers huddled & I left early enough to pass for an uninvited guest, a kind of music then—the sound of the approaching soldiers: their boots, almost broken in.

To say in dreams wanting redemption the dead return, to say an upturned collar against the wind retracing the same weather patterns, to say the same reluctance to call the landscape anything but consistent, to say consistency is a virtue, to claim a kinship to what one can't control, to call the clouds themselves an outline of their own possibilities, to posit anything as fact, as the fiction of a self-subsistent egalitarian peach orchard, to organize a blizzard from the blossoms, to boast about a ray of sun from the rain, to leave it just left of the lens, to call elision an inevitability, a lack of crows in the foreground, to feign composure when someone's weeping, to call it fine weather whether or not one's left the house, the hill, the hand that couldn't help pulling the strings a little tighter, to say a taut line's sure to turn up ample fish forgetting one's already eaten, to find the tunnel leading from the sublime to the stasis of countless layers of oil paint, to call in the crows, the crying stranger, the dead & their dancing party, partly to pull the lens a little left of the landscape, partly to latch onto the larger motifs, Mount Fuji, my free hand, my finite sense of closure already spinning in the waterwheels, wearing its brightest white costume, sure to soak up all the blood you'd ever need.

I'm not chronicling in camphor & stilts, not washed out with the sights, slants bending irrevocably inward, above the hills, past an old flag post. Is this psychic automatism in its pure state, or merely a different route for the same daily walk? Abundant flower parts lacking a precise analogy? Years unwinding smaller years, ending an argument? Two thin triangles of breath across the windowpane. There's no bargaining when the horse wants in.

If it's serious motion we're talking about, let's talk about serious motion. The tanker leaves without a horizon to back it and a line of birds shoots the scene with something of a hum. Can't you handle the pace built from such a deep backtracking? Outside the wood, another wood, less dense. Less concerned with the passing of time, with enough bricks to rebuild the blank spots the city called to itself. If the lime tree wasn't there after the storm, nor the scent of burnt leaves, if stalemates stalled the chamber door & I'm cooking less these days, then it's an odd clock face, an abstract trust to watch the smaller hand insist on working its way through the round world. Cars passed continually. Beyond the trees, more trees. Past those, a month without gears.

Not that my tangent knife cuts into any book's ending, but why are there so many bucket dents in the darkroom, so many ways to be emulsified. The army hums. The jets hum. The houses hum & no one rides them anymore. So the musket patch might not bury me, but it's a subtle truth for a shark tooth collector. I wouldn't doubt the cabinets were wholly lacking in noise, in the ostentatious nothing I'm turning on here, the sort of mythic immediacy lacking in so many real stories. It's obvious under fluorescent light. What wouldn't be?

So the waves brought the boat to a slant & I didn't have time to look for someone else to ferry, to scan the ads, move this orange tank closer to an absent future. I'd call it the spot where a statue should be set. Here, among leftover footprints, or the lack of footprints. It's a sorry drill sergeant who sends letters when sleep might wane, when the moon shadow makes you scoff at another discharge tenant, disregarding the tent stakes & iron rations. It's not quite a question to turn the transistor stick over to its rightful owner. If day floats down in a subservient shuffling & the teabags tear & you can't read the news right anyhow, then who's to say a bee farmer won't make flower noise in the haystacks. It's all frizzled glaze, the chime takers & the chime tellers.

When no one writes from the red city walls & it's cold in the vault, a torn compass & a few doomed flowers leave me about as bare as wheat, lifting droll tones, leaning in vehemently. It's enough to pass without looking for the dayrot, without turning off the television, finding a clicking underneath, covering it in a dull, ginger-gold haze. The cord crackles, holds a sliver of the light it takes to unlace someone from the balcony. A brown shirt in the wind makes a bad memory box & all this walking & unwalking is a haunting way to tell a ghost she can't come home.

1/03–5/03

THE AREA OF SOUND CALLED THE SUBTONE

I began to play a few musical airs which I myself had invented...
All my troubles stemmed from there.
—Erik Satie

Oh yes we need this new sound.
My heartball sing the real gospel's in town.
—H.R.

i. gray matter migration zone

Look! a hand—the palm, blue. The back-lit
bones, shown through an x-ray. They're zero
ing in: cloning / cloning. There's a sheep in the shop,
a dust cloud in the film. Someone stood overlooking; someone
still against a tree. The rays, soft & dropping.
The choppers are chopping a raincoat—the
fabric where an elbow pokes through.
The socket drains & in draining, the metallic-blue mercury
follows the spectrum to a flame's tip: fire burns,
that is the first law. Then the sound left—it gone.
& in far other scenes! say, the evacuation area.
Or, the hive: they're in hysterics—a scattering of ants.
Each lifts a larva as the alarm rings, spiraling down,
filling the passage way—the sound!

sound. the passageway they're filling
with thunder grown from sheet metal's violent shake.
a bi-coastal broadcast: down with the ship, the war
with Eurasia & what the Shadow knows: static in the subtones.
they scamper from under the sound as though from a stone overturned.
moving outward, they dissipate; move & declare: motion, a void.
the declaration: an opening as ground or glass is broken.
a hole. a tear. the threadbare hopes of a complementary de
coder ring. decoding, a roomful of chimps types away.
microprocessors map the DNA of a black dot. scanning
the Song of Songs for what it actually says. the way sub
tones wear their architecture like an old coat,
an unraveled rope—its threads, undone,
so put up the scythe: they're splitting the atom.

Adam's split. Psych! the input they've
put in was all wrong. Past the garden, a train passing
a silo of rotting grain. & the tea—waterlogged
& tossed over the side. Curving around
the milk-white corpse of each dawn, daybreak
& evening, the lines looped back to the bunker like
moonlight or a light cover of ash
& they drank in the nexus. Or, in
Dublin, injecting oranges with vodka via a syringe.
Bed sheets, tied end-on-end toward the failure of candy w/ a fizz:
an allure, children pulsing through the brain-case.
The shop windows, blown out! already, a few moments before
the drop. (key of D) // here's what opens
the aperture, the temple's door, the camera's lens.

iv. they're paving the streets with crushed glass

a lens pans past the door, tightens the aperture to
a solitary drop of rain contained in an icicle:
a single cancerous cell & every grain of sand, realigned
until a footprint appears. here, the metal detector's beams
ricochet from a rusting key—the soot-stained flint of entry
or the fireplace where one spark flitters
upward, like a hand reaching toward
the chimney's open flue, tumbles & rights itself
& re-falls—& does not cease, falling & re
falling with a roar, a refraction of light.
was it light within? stillness becoming alive as
an unwound rope, a dissipating orbit marking the
plunge—the soft blue. a star, affixing its beam while
the emperor steps on a crack in the ice's seam.

v. the death of the alleyway

Seems nice there in back. The dropped temper of a
transistor radio, signals of black & curling subtones dis
solving into static, fingertips run along the curtains—
the automatic thump. A train passing through the chest,
its low rumble beneath the ribs & a fire-escape, ten
feet from the sidewalk. Then, flattened—a coin, an empty
well. Trace its contours like a
body rotting in the rushes—the may butterfly's penultimate place.
A full plastic bag. Not a twist-tie. The hand's grip,
indifferent to knotted sheets, to the mashed-in moon.
Light shown off a hilt; the blade—buried. A dog
stopped at the river's edge; its head, cocked toward the sound
of a sinking stone—tossed from among the trees—toward
the reflected flux of light, of what a leaf's underside sees.

vi. solar eclipse in D minor

seen underneath without light, free & refracting the
ward of night's electric stripes. there's a hoop on fire,
a halo of water radiating outward in rings; each,
the demand for rope & someone to man the riggings
like the jagged line of light from between every stone.
the sand holds the imprint of passing as an engine in the sky, the
sky cut across by the exhaust's
needle: the concrete gray of fulfillment, diminished—
a hollowed-out vein! *the shop are narrow but shops is long.*
the landscape, outlined by telephone poles,
drawn toward their wooden faces. a worn anvil under the mirrored
crown, its showering of sparks, & a train
gathering distance, illuminating rails; they falter,
collecting as though they're drops of water.

Water? Water everywhere! Although the drops collect
to form a body—here, a hallway: dark puddles of wine,
the rouge of a mouth. Three black birds take off
from a tree like a drone circling the queen's brain-case,
etching the new stories into her ear-hole. No sound of it here
but with the wind! The temple, a vessel one leads toward,
more than pressure & the wall's thinness,
more than innocent cruelty, but more away.
Frequencies, wobbling the radio. The radio, in flames.
The west window shut off; its screen sucked to a black dot.
Waves, succumbing while the television displays snow.
A piano key struck: the momentary twitchings & again
darkness. The night's tenor, its hollowed-out book,
back-lit. The blue palm, the hand—a look!

a bomb? a word = the truth in things other
than subtones burning a hole in the ozone or passing through
the brain-case & out an ear-hole. the fire has blue legs, shoes
like rain. on Sundays, the barber sang in the choir while
his narrow shop was closed. an interlude played on
the organ. it pushing out air. each pulse,
more than pressure & the wall's thinness
keeping a voice from traveling too far. the broom
grew from a bare stem as a body does from a skeleton
or a movement from a set of tics. worn marble
on the stairs & the statuary greening. footsteps led from
the sound of a scale moving upward. lead was removed from the walls.
some such phrase as "ideas should be the sound of a thing"
which means, that is, sings: music is nothing.

ix. it's true!—the notes have feet

Nothing in music sings in that means which
sets a metronome to dreaming of its return
to the womb, or the waves from
responding to the moon's cyclonic fury, the fire,
the leaden flood & finally the cost—bombers
circling twice before returning home, while the
sky, cut across by the exhaust's
thin white finger, splits in two.
A back & the hollow body of a well's litany of stone.
The ledge where the panel's shown in the still rise of water
settling to feel out the contours like flesh filling out bone.
A red umbrella raised to the unwound moon; its rays—
a fugue in the neck! & evening's unmoored; it's gone higher
than the landscape rewound to a field where all flames afire.

x. succumbing to the black dot

a fire flares the worn field of an interior landscape.

                                                        it answers:

        7. work always in streaks

      10. what about letters received, use of sun lamp

      13. gland hurts

a shadow in the mirror & a tendril poking through.

well, trace its contours, like a

seagull—/   <u>keep circling</u>:

      22. horror of random noise

      43. afraid of being localized in space

distance——

      the loss of space,   blanketing like ash,

a mirror's indifference.

      borders inherent in the word: fence

xi. how even snow can settle on a steeple

Since when? Thinning, the boundaries tore
across a stain of white in the hallway, where
behind a door, the radio kept blaring: them raining fire again…
Then, static—white noise. White of the moth. White of
the face rubbed from a coin. Not moving
upward like a hand reaching
toward someone in the room. The radio, bleeping: "Ambrose, Ambrose"
bleeping: *Ambrose*. Subtones circling like an overwhelming question.
Eye. Iris. Isotope. & in which meaning, what is it? & in
which wave, it's it—what it is? How the sound, traveling, was called
run off. & the manual read: MELTDOWN WARNING
The siren's soft blue light like money buried in the backyard.
Revealed in an x-ray, the transparent elasticity
opening both inward & outward—toxins in the body.

embodying the offer, thought wading in, warding both openings—
the casing of a shell, bullets held in a rotating strip, fit for
28 hours straight until night scattered along its edges
as though across the screen. & a scampering be-
tween walls was heard & blinds were pulled &
storm shutters placed on shelters now under
moonlight or a light cover of ash,
of what hovers above the field, framed:
the idea of space as a vessel / a fire escape, the boat.
buoyancy became the predicate to a lifetime of blueprints
mapped out in a basement. an abandoned shout for someone
a violent luck & a whole sample. the sun, an incessant thump;
check the watch. their scalps—check the children.
a violin! the way a spoon conducts the skin of men!

xiii. evolution of the origin of matter

Om the head of a pin: heat, conducted via a spoon:
the violin, dissolving sound: an untuned string or a stage direction:

> *evening sky*
> *2nd story window:*
> *(enter blue)*

as in the air settling in the space between buildings.
The declaration: an opening. As ground or glass is broken,
so with the cooling, so be it—the core! a slow weather. The weight
in each word recovered. There were screw holes meant for framing:
the signs, painted yellow & black. & the amount of notes
pitched out in a breath, the saxophone's river—its depth:
there was a city here.   here there was a city!   was there a city here?
They could see what had once been Main Street from beneath the lake.
...*we're going down!...down...we're going down for Christ's sake!*

taken. curved. flung down. worse? down! gone where?
two syllables of comfort from a charred box. all lost.
in the market, the fire. it wild, stained.
the trees went blue, bleating. the public architecture, dropped.
how a needle cuts into each groove,
echoed in the song about a raincoat—the
fabric where an elbow pokes through:
them raining fire again, them got to run,
from Babylon for I & I them choppers come
flammable, scattered—the table-strewn blueprints.
at the bottom &—a hand unfolds. drawn across.
& a breath, smoke. huddled in the doorway:
a ghost? a rat? the door? some
other things are true: the word, *bomb*.

6/01—7/01

ABOUT THE AUTHOR

Noah Eli Gordon was born in Cleveland, Ohio, in 1975. Author of the book-length poem *The Frequencies,* published in 2003, his poetry and reviews have appeared in numerous journals and in chapbooks from Duration Press, Margin to Margin, Anchorite, and Anon Books. He currently lives in Northampton, Massachussets, where he publishes the Braincase chapbook series.

Ahsahta Press

SAWTOOTH POETRY PRIZE SERIES

2002: AARON McCOLLOUGH, *Welkin* (Brenda Hillman, judge)
2003: GRAHAM FOUST, *Leave the Room to Itself* (Joe Wenderoth, judge)
2004: NOAH ELI GORDON, *The Area of Sound Called the Subtone* (Claudia Rankine, judge)

NEW SERIES

DAN BEACHY-QUICK, *Spell*
LISA FISHMAN, *Dear, Read*
PEGGY HAMILTON, *Forbidden City*
CHARLES O. HARTMAN, *Island*
LANCE PHILLIPS, *Corpus Socius*
LANCE PHILLIPS, *Cur aliquid vidi*
HEATHER SELLERS, *Drinking Girls and Their Dresses*
LIZ WALDNER, *Saving the Appearances*

MODERN AND CONTEMPORARY POETRY OF THE AMERICAN WEST

SANDRA ALCOSSER, *A Fish to Feed All Hunger*
DAVID AXELROD, *Jerusalem of Grass*
DAVID BAKER, *Laws of the Land*
DICK BARNES, *Few and Far Between*
CONGER BEASLEY, JR., *Over DeSoto's Bones*
LINDA BIERDS, *Flights of the Harvest-Mare*
RICHARD BLESSING, *Winter Constellations*
BOYER, BURMASTER, AND TRUSKY, EDS., *The Ahsahta Anthology*
PEGGY POND CHURCH, *New and Selected Poems*

KATHARINE COLES, *The One Right Touch*

WYN COOPER, *The Country of Here Below*

CRAIG COTTER, *Chopstix Numbers*

JUDSON CREWS, *The Clock of Moss*

H.L. DAVIS, *Selected Poems*

SUSAN STRAYER DEAL, *The Dark is a Door*

SUSAN STRAYER DEAL, *No Moving Parts*

LINDA DYER, *Fictional Teeth*

GRETEL EHRLICH, *To Touch the Water*

GARY ESAREY, *How Crows Talk and Willows Walk*

JULIE FAY, *Portraits of Women*

THOMAS HORNSBY FERRIL, *Anvil of Roses*

THOMAS HORNSBY FERRIL, *Westering*

HILDEGARDE FLANNER, *The Hearkening Eye*

CHARLEY JOHN GREASYBEAR, *Songs*

CORRINNE HALES, *Underground*

HAZEL HALL, *Selected Poems*

NAN HANNON, *Sky River*

GWENDOLEN HASTE, *Selected Poems*

KEVIN HEARLE, *Each Thing We Know Is Changed Because We Know It And Other Poems*

SONYA HESS, *Kingdom of Lost Waters*

CYNTHIA HOGUE, *The Woman in Red*

ROBERT KRIEGER, *Headlands, Rising*

ELIO EMILIANO LIGI, *Disturbances*

HANIEL LONG, *My Seasons*

KEN MCCULLOUGH, *Sycamore•Oriole*

NORMAN MCLEOD, *Selected Poems*

BARBARA MEYN, *The Abalone Heart*

DAVID MUTSCHLECNER, *Esse*

DIXIE PARTRIDGE, *Deer in the Haystacks*

GERRYE PAYNE, *The Year-God*

GEORGE PERREAULT, *Curved Like an Eye*

HOWARD W. ROBERTSON, *to the fierce guard in the Assyrian Saloon*

LEO ROMERO, *Agua Negra*

This book is set in Apollo type with ITC Officina Sans titles
by Ahsahta Press at Boise State University
and manufactured on acid-free paper
by Boise State University Printing and Graphics, Boise, Idaho.

AHSAHTA PRESS

2004

JANET HOLMES, DIRECTOR

SCOTT ABELS JOHN OTTEY
J. REUBEN APPELMAN ERICH SCHWEIKHER
SANDY FRIEDLY AMY WEGNER
WENDY GREEN MARY HICKMAN, INTERN
KAREN MOYER AMY GARRETT, INTERN
BRANDON NOLTA MIA WRIGHT, INTERN